Imagems 3

By Richard Berengarten

SELECTED WRITINGS : SHEARSMAN EDITION
Vol. 1   *For the Living : Selected Longer Poems, 1965–2000*
Vol. 2   *The Manager*
Vol. 3   *The Blue Butterfly* (Part 1, *The Balkan Trilogy*)
Vol. 4   *In a Time of Drought* (Part 2, *The Balkan Trilogy*)
Vol. 5   *Under Balkan Light* (Part 3, *The Balkan Trilogy*)
Vol. 6   *Manual : the first hundred*
Vol. 7   *Notness : Metaphysical Sonnets*
Vol. 8   *Changing*
Vol. 9   *A Portrait in Inter-Views*
Vol. 10 *Balkan Spaces : Essays and Prose-Pieces*

OTHER POETRY
Avebury
The Easter Rising 1967
The Return of Lazarus
Double Flute
Inhabitable Space
Some Poems, Illuminated by Frances Richards
Learning to Talk
Roots/Routes
Half of Nowhere
Against Perfection
Book With No Back Cover
DYAD, with Will Hill

OTHER PROSE
Keys to Transformation : Ceri Richards and Dylan Thomas
Imagems (1)
Imagems (2)

AS EDITOR
An Octave for Octavio Paz
Ceri Richards : Drawings to Poems by Dylan Thomas
Rivers of Life
In Visible Ink : Selected Poems, Roberto Sanesi, 1955–1979
Homage to Mandelstam
Out of Yugoslavia
For Angus
The Perfect Order : Selected Poems, Nasos Vayenas, 1974–2010
IDEA and ACT

Imagems 3

Richard Berengarten

Shearsman Books

First published in the United Kingdom in 2025 by
Shearsman Books Ltd
PO Box 4239
Swindon SN3 9FN

Shearsman Books Ltd Registered Office
30–31 St. James Place, Mangotsfield, Bristol BS16 9JB
(this address not for correspondence)

EU AUTHORISED REPRESENTATIVE:
Lightning Source France, 1 Av. Johannes Gutenberg,
78310 Maurepas, France   Email: compliance@lightningsource.fr

www.shearsman.com

ISBN 978-1-84861-907-4

ACKNOWLEDGEMENTS

My thanks to the editors of the following for publishing versions of some
of these texts : 'Poetry, Trees, and Hope' and 'A Dendrology : On Language
and Trees' (2016–2017) appeared online in *Margutte* in English and Italian
(trans./ed. Silvia Pio) ; 'Imaginationalism', in English and Chinese (trans.
Chen Shangzhen) in the Kulangsu (*aka* Gulangyu) International Poetry
Festival programme, Xiamen, China (2016) ; 'On the Spirit of Poetry in a
Time of Plague' (2020), in *Fortnightly Review* online and on the *Medellín
International Poetry Festival* website ; 'Riddling the Riddle', in *Riddles
and Spells / Devinettes et sorts* (trans./ed. Geneviève Guetemme), Orléans,
Corsaire Éditions (2024) ; and 'Poetry and Midnight : Approaching the
Hour', 'On Poetry and Dream', and 'Poetry and Midnight : Chiming the
Hour', in *Cambridge Poetry*, Episode 1 (2024). My profound thanks to Paul
Scott Derrick, Anthony Rudolf and my wife, Melanie Rein, for their critical
suggestions on a near-final draft of this text. The cover shows a sketch of
the author made by Marin Sorescu in Belgrade, 1982, as do the covers of
Imagems I and *Imagems 2* (Shearsman Books, 2013 and 2019, respectively).

Contents

…& every Minute Particular is Holy…

WILLIAM BLAKE

… ἔστι may roughly be expressed by *things are* or *there is truth*. Grammatically it = *it is* or *there is*. But indeed I have often felt when I have been in this mood and felt the depth of an instress or how fast the inscape holds a thing that nothing is so pregnant and straightforward to the truth as simple *yes* and *is*.

GERARD MANLEY HOPKINS

Poised at the point of midnight, without heeding the breath of hours, the poet divests himself of all that is unnecessary in life, experiencing the abstract ambivalence of being and nonbeing.

GASTON BACHELARD

In my craft or sullen art
Exercised in the still night …

DYLAN THOMAS

I imagine this midnight moment's forest …

TED HUGHES

Poetry and Midnight

Approaching the Hour

1. As midnight approaches, not sleep but poetry beckons.

2. The heart speeds. Pores open. Darkness, a black fire, billows shadows that swallow you. Shadows inside shadows. Shadows overlapping shadows. Until black is total. And no more pluralities.

3. But out of this – *letters*! They swell in gradual negative, whitely on black fire. Elegantly, they shape. Into a swirl of alphabets. Into a stream of characters. Awash, flooded, engulfed. Scratched, carved, scalpelled. Pitted, painted, printed.

4. Their forms drift along, about. They touch, graze, jostle. They bump into one another. Some rebound, some open borders, some get swallowed up. Some merge, meld.

5. No danger here. Only act and pass on. Only action and passion. Building, binding, breeding. The letters clutch, agglomerate. A bunch, a bundle, a cluster. This gathers, grows, glues. Then compresses, condenses.

6. It fans into a sound. The sound forms a syllable. Tapered at each end.

7. It repeats clearly. More clearly. Syllables catch breaths.

8. Matter – worlds of matter – haven't yet begun to be. What might be material hasn't yet broken or spoken.

9. A poem begins to write you, write itself, write itself out, right out of you.

10. As from rock, carved letters, Or blazing, spilling, flowing, out of a volcano's heart. Now down-flowing, incessantly down.

11. Did you once contain *blood* ? Whatever *you* was, or might have been, *before* is a spattered husk. *You* has been utterly voided. *You*, quitted, acquitted.

12. A half-made thing half-emerges. Will this be a poem ? You'll find out when you get back to it. When you put yourself back together. Quieted, you drift off.

Imaginationalism

Twelve actualities

1. For the last fifty years, my poetic practice been international. As well as living in England, my birth-land, I've lived in Greece, Italy, the USA and former Yugoslavia. My books have been inspired by the literatures, cultures, histories, and psycho-geographies of all these places.

2. *Changing* (2016) is a homage to the cultural, poetic and philosophical traditions of China. This book is grounded in the *I Ching* (*Yijing, Book of Changes*). Even though I'm an English speaker and know only a little of the Chinese language, *Changing* entirely depends on and derives from this ancient Chinese masterpiece. How is this possible ?

3. Through its translations and the commentaries on it in languages other than Chinese, the *I Ching* has become not only one of the finest treasures of Chinese tradition but a possession that belongs to all humanity. So if a linguistic purist were to argue, "Since you don't speak Chinese, you can't even read, let alone understand the *I Ching*," my reply would be : "I can read and understand the Bible, but I don't know ancient Hebrew, Aramaic or Greek. The King James *Authorised Version* (1611) is a masterpiece in itself."

4. Clearly, then, the importance of translation throughout the world of poetry can't be underestimated, despite all the distortions and misinterpretations any translation inevitably risks, even the most faithful. Today, thanks to translations, *all* cultural, literary and poetic traditions in the world are open, accessible and available to *us all*, part of our rightful and meaningful human heritage.

5. So a Chinese poet today can be influenced by, say, the *Epic of Gilgamesh*, Keats, Rimbaud, Tsvetaeva, Celan – just as I, an

English poet, can be influenced by Homer, Tao Yuanming, Paz, Seferis and Lalić. What vistas are open !

6.   We're all territorial *and* extra-territorial. Chinese-speakers can be found in most major cities in the world. So can speakers of Greek, Albanian, Swahili, Bengali, and hundreds of other languages, large and small. Every culture, at least potentially, has its *diaspora* (seed-spreading). And every language is international. And if that's the case, then so is (its) poetry.

7.   So the issue of what's 'native' and what's 'foreign' in poetry needs rephrasing. An apple tree can grow just as well in an orchard in Sichuan as in Normandy, Illinois or Buenos Aires, and the taste of its fruit can be just as individual and sweet. The world is as full of cultural reseedings and linguistic transferences as of botanical transplantations.

8.   So, for a poet to be open to linguistic and literary influences other than those within his/her own ancestral heritage never needs to imply loss of personal or cultural identity, but rather enrichment, widening, deepening.

9.   All literatures are part of one literature ; all poetries, part of one poetry. All human cultures belong together and cohere.

10.   We're all part of the deep, wide running current William Wordsworth called the "music of humanity".

11.   So, whatever its label may be, the age both of present-day poetry and of poetry-to-come is irreducibly and inevitably transcultural, multilingual, international.

12.   I call this *imaginational.*

On Poetry and Dream

Twelve propositions

1. The closer I am to dream when awake, the more quickly and clearly the poem moves and breathes in and through me. Upwards and outwards : spring-like. Purer, wilder, wiser. Inwards and downwards : autumnal. Both equally pure, wild, wise – and equally beautiful. And both, drenched in mortality. The dream, like the poem, both comments on and criticises both living and dying.[1] Do dreams and poems also *rehearse* dying ? *And* living ?

2. Is any dream ever finalised, finished, final ? Isn't there's always more in the dream to be dreamed ? More *to* the dream. An *elseness* that always lies further, farther than any *this-here-now* ? In this unfinishment, and in the intuition or apperception of it, lies an implicit *if only* – if not of a given futurity, then of (a) longing – and, perhaps, even, of (a) possibility. This elseness resides precisely in the being of *if only* belonging further elsewhere, farther elsewhen. I can't help waking up, can I ? But a dream may be re-dreamed or continued, through and past wakeness – into another dream.

3. Whoever thinks being awake means deploying the fullest range, height and depth of the human mind entertains a belief that needs, at least, more questioning, more examining, more challenging. For how can any such belief contain any more than an inkling of truth, when waking and wakeness necessarily and inevitably involve the huge – even total – forgetting and forgetfulness of the dream, of all its possessions and precisions, its multiple meanings, memories and intimations, its compendia of treasures and temptations ?

4. The dream embeds and roots my personal mind, my consciousness – no, not *just* mind, not *just* consciousness, but surely, my entire being – right back into its sleepy primeval origins, into their undercurrents and undertows, and their reflections and reversals. In the dream, my mind, my consciousness, my being itself sinks

down, through its roots, to taste its root-nourishments – mineral, vegetal, and archetypal. And down there, *sometimes* – in times that aren't *times* at all – an archetype may assault me, seep into me, invest in me, soaking me in images. And, if and when that happens down there, in the archaic ache of the archetype, eternity itself also tempts, radiates, glimmers.

5. What best and most effectively *re-members* the dream, puts its limbs back into it, and enables it to move again through me ? What most resonantly and resolutely *re-calls* it and most plausibly *re-stores* and *re-patterns* it, at least partly, to its originary being, in and through me ? In and through the medium of language, this capacity is the poem's. And even though the poem that emerges from (out of) the dream isn't its finishment, or its perfectment, and still less its copy, it *is* its continuation and its regeneration. Its child. Its offspring. And equally, its *Perle* !²

6. Dear Prospero, take me into it with you. Dear Donne, remember to call me up, so I can follow you, even accompany you. Dear Master Oyster, do likewise when you accrete another *Perle* around – *what* ? – a sandgrain ? Or like Blake, witness an entire world inside that core.

7. The dream purrs, pours, prowls through the poem. Its sighs, soars, sears through every part. It sings, strikes, rages, rings. It roars, whispers, hums. It drums, beats, batters, betters. It hints, suggests, intimates.

8. A dream *verbs* and keeps on *verbing*. It *nouns* and keeps on *nouning*. A dream is *eventmental*. It is even an *event*. It is even *and* an event, even though it may be no event at all, but a drift of, in and through vaguest haze. And in the dream – just as every verb *nouns* itself – so also, equally and reciprocally, every noun *verbs* itself. And that, at least partly, is how the dream inspires and evokes a poem. As an inkling, a sprinkling, a straining. An inking, a marking, a staining. These are only faint clues about how the

poem lives, how it's destined, how designed, how made. How it's born – in, through and out of the dream.

9. And so many dreams of *people* : known and unknown, recognised and never before seen, alive or ghosted but brought back ! And so many speaking in their own authentic voices ! And as for animals, so many, too ! Last night a scorpion. Tonight, an elephant ? Next, a lizard, a louse, a leopard ? A damsel-fly, a dragonfly, a dragon ? The one and only Phoenix ? The dream keeps *animalling*, it keeps on *souling* and *ensouling* – insistently, as its people and animals appear, wake, speak.[3] Hmm, I can't help this. Can I ? No, I can't. And won't – even if I don't understand it myself. Here beginneth the poem.

10. *And* so many plants and plantings, intermingling, chimæra-like ! Huge plantations of lions. Wild herds of trees and shrubs. Deep forests of bees. Jungles of spiralling herring. Shoals of firs and pines. Orgies of plankton. Hives of sedges and ferns. Trees, tubers, trees. Swarms and swarms of seeds. Hordes and hordes of flowers. Of every shape and colour imaginable. The force that through the green fuse drives the tiger.

11. What a miserable existence it would be to have no poems. Almost as disastrous as being bereft of dreams. Might it be possible to really live, having no dreams at all ?

12. In both dream and poem *I* simply isn't I. The *I* is I no longer. But a dream of *I* through and by me. By and through me entrained. By and through me entranced.

On the Spirit of Poetry in a Time of Plague

The First Imaginationalist Manifesto

1. COVID, if I catch and carry it, may bring not only my own sickness, sorrow, suffering, and possibly death, but also those of another, of others. COVID can destroy my health, haleness, wellness, life itself, and those of another, others, many others. As an agent and carrier of death, COVID can literally *take my breath away* – and yours, one *you* or more *you*.

2. COVID is both individual and communal. Individual, because if I catch it, it's *I* who suffer. Communal, because it's infectious, i.e. capable of being carried to me only by another (others) and equally to another (others) by me. I don't, won't, can't catch COVID in any other way than from somebody else, some other body. Nor do, will, can you : *you* singular, *you* plural.

3. COVID makes me realise and recognise more and more deeply that I'm mortal, that (my) life is short, that (my) nature is animal, that (my) death is inevitable, ineluctable, inescapable – and that all this is true of and for you too – again, *you* singular and *you* plural.

4. Nor can I avoid converting all the above statements, which refer to *I* and *me*, to all other pronouns (beings and entities) – above all to, *you*, singular, *other*, and *you*, plural, *others* : that is, all together, *we* / *us*. COVID can't help personalising, individualising *everybody*, each and every *anybody* or *somebody*, any and every *other*, all *others*. But curiously, far from separating us, COVID emphasises our community and, perhaps, even *creates* our communality, which is inevitably universal, since nobody (human), even if inoculated, can be entirely excluded from the risk of catching this plague.

5. All these areas of attentivity involves my realisation, too, that so far as I (we, all of us) know, *there's no consciousness without mortality*.

6.   Poetry is the linguistic medium above all others and *par excellence* that not only bares this entire set of awarenesses of mortality but also enables me (us, all of us) to bear it, and to do so with courage, patience, modesty, and compassion for others.

7.   So : in such times as this time, this time of plague, I (we, you) rely on poetry more and more, and with increasing curiosity, urgency and passion. For poems, including stories and songs, are more capable of forming, formulating, expressing and communicating care, carefulness, and caringness – *and* doing so more honestly, truthfully, intensely, fully and profoundly, than any other linguistic expression.

8.   Conversely, when any expression in language touches, even grazes – even so much as hints at – any such quality of honesty, truthfulness, intensity, fulness and profundity, it necessarily becomes poetry.

9.   For that's precisely what poetry is : language in its highest, best and completest form of honesty, truthfulness, intensity and profundity.

10. So I (you, we, all of us) need, want, rely on poetry in a time of plague, not only because it *consoles* me (all of you, all of us) – in, through and despite all my (our, your) weaknesses and fragilities – but also because it makes me (us) even more aware of all these aspects of living and dying. In so doing, it brings me (each of you, each of us) closer to the realities of the human heart, mind, spirit, soul, flesh, body.

11. But poetry isn't expressive of only pain and suffering. Poetry is and brings and reveals joy, *and* hope, *and* courage in the *thisness*, the *hereness*, the *nowness* of the *this-here-now*, in the miraculous beauty and grace of this universe in the fullest possible context of all its (and our) mornings and evenings, nights and days, morrows and tomorrows.

12. With respect to and within the specific field of *language*, in the face of birth and death – this face that is so clearly delineated in a time of plague – poetry is the prime and most treasured agent of all hope, all courage, all joy.

Poetry, Trees, and Hope

Twelve Propositions

1. Our words *inspiration*, *respiration* and *spirit* all have origin in the Latin verb *spirare* 'to breathe'.

2. We breathe involuntarily and necessarily. The air we depend on for life itself surrounds the earth like a mantle. As it covers and protects the earth and all life on earth, so equally the air belongs to the earth and all of earth's creatures, including humans. The air is both ours and not ours. My air and your air are one.

3. Trees enable us to breathe. Because our air has constantly renewed itself for millions of years, until very recently we have assumed it's limitless. But now the great forests are in danger of being killed off, and we know our supply of oxygen may itself be threatened. Half of this supply depends on the photosynthesis performed by trees, shrubs, grasses, and other plants. Our mantle of air, which should be inalienable from our earth, is polluted, worn, fragile.

4. Some trees may live for hundreds, even thousands of years. So to plant and care for trees helps to secure (safeguard, ensure, insure, guarantee, conserve) the supply and flow of oxygen we need for our breath(ing) now and in future, for the breath(ing) of our children and our children's children, and for our descendants down through multiple generations.

5. To plant and care for trees presupposes belief and investment in futurity. Which is to say : to plant and care for trees is *action rooted in hope*. Whoever protects, nurtures and nourishes trees is a guardian of the future. The job of a guardian is to guard and guide. Tree-planters and tree-tenders are guardians of our future gardens, our future's gardens.

6. Poems are born, rooted, and routed in and through breath. A poet's inspiration is both personal, because it's his or her very own, and transpersonal, because inspiration itself flows to, into and through the poet from sources that are other, outside. A poet is a maker (Scots, *makar*) who marks his or her own personal speech with inner inspiration. A true (authentic) poem is personal speech marked by inspiration, which renders it both personal and transpersonal at once. Hence, also : a poem is speech that transfers (transmits, transports) its maker's (makar's) inner inspiration to a reader or listener on and through a thread of words that are inspired.

7. A poem may live as long as a tree, and often far longer. Once made, a living poem may transmit inspiration to multiple generations of readers, many of whom may not be alive until centuries after its maker has died. A poem and its meanings may travel – *and* unravel – rolling, unrolling, unscrolling – across time and across (over, around, past, beyond) many individual deaths, including that of the poet in, through and from whom it originated.

8. No true poet would write for his or her generation alone. A poet necessarily makes poems for an unknown reader who may or may not be alive now – and if not now, who will be, one day, in a time and place unknown. The claim of any true poet is necessarily that of Shakespeare, that his/her own poem will live as "long as men can breathe or eyes can see" (Sonnet 18). This is also the claim staked by the Russian poet Osip Mandelstam, in slightly different terms : "Maybe, for these lines to reach their addressee, it will take the same hundreds of years that it does for the light of a planet to reach another planet." And Mandelstam adds, "[P]oetry as a whole is always directed at a more or less distant, unknown addressee, in whose existence the poet may not doubt without doubting himself."[4]

9. So, making and reading poetry, like the planting and care of trees, necessarily invokes both futurity and hope. Anthony Rudolf reminds us : "Poetry presupposes future, presupposes continuity." And in amplifying this idea, he adds : "The poem is an implicit

guarantor of the good life ; it insists upon the life beyond itself."[5]
Consisting of language, made in language – made in *a* particular
language and inhabiting it, a poem, then, *looks forward* in both
meanings of this phrase. And here, the phrase "the life beyond
itself" can scarcely fail to mean (signify, indicate, point to,
denote, want to say) anything or anyone other than *the life of an
other*, of *the other* : the perpetual *you*. The poem looks out *to* and
for you-out-there, whoever you are or may be, to bring you *here*,
into here, into now.

10. Nature, with its infinite variety and distribution of life-forms and
     patterns, is an ever-brimming, over-brimming, self-replenishing
     fountain of inspiration for poetry. Or so we believe and hope,
     and so we aim to keep making true. Conversely, many poems
     that inspire us most simply and immediately, most directly and
     deeply, are often those that connect us to the natural world – that
     is to say, to the *isness* of what is, in all its mysterious simplicity
     and complexity combined : in all its *just-so-ness*. So, not only does
     our caring for the natural world guard, care for and nurture the
     source(s) of our future inspiration, but poetry reciprocally guards,
     cares for and nurtures the natural world, by encouraging humans
     to love, respect and protect this animated world.

11. Our poetic (mythopoeic) way of perceiving and knowing
     the world, and our ecological advocacy and defence of the
     green world, are one and the same : connected, wise, old, and
     ever-young. What we recognise as ecological necessity must
     (necessarily) include poetry. For just as certain species of trees
     belong in all countries of the world, so certain species of poems
     belong in all languages. And just as trees that are native to a
     particular terrain may be transplanted (translated), to thrive in
     other soils, so the many-branched patterns and paths of poetry
     must include translation too.

12. The guardianship of trees and the making and receiving of poems
     intertwine along the paths we follow as we make our way, whether
     gradually and gracefully, or in jumps and starts, towards cosmic
     consciousness. As trees are the mothers of our breath, inspiration
     is the mother of hope.

A Dendrology : On Language and Trees

Twelve propositions

1. The word *anthology* means a 'collection of poems'. This usage blends two ideas : a 'gathering of flowers' and a 'gathering of extracts from writings'.[6] In other words, an anthology is conceived as a kind of finely arranged bouquet of words, ideas and concepts. The idea that ideas, expressed in language, can have the qualities of flowers (their forms, shapes, colours and perfumes) is itself fine. And beautiful.

2. The botanical origin of the word *anthology* plausibly suggests an appropriate analogical extension and variation : a *dendrology*.[7] The meaning of this word, which is usually "the study of trees" or "the department of botany which treats of trees",[8] I extend here to mean a 'gathering or collection of tree-poems'.

3. The dendrology inaugurated by this text in the online journal *Margutte* advocates, celebrates, defends and upholds the lives and presences of both trees and poems.[9] The implicit claim it offers (and now makes explicit) is that in doing just that, it also advocates, celebrates, defends, and upholds the organic diversity of human languages.

4. Languages are comparable to biological species in several distinct but related ways. Each individual language is unique, irreplaceable, *special, specific*. Like species, languages belong to families : they originate, and assume their shapes and forms mysteriously, both phylogenetically and ontogenetically ; they develop, mature, and die ; they shift, flit, and get blown about, in, on, and by the wind ; they jump ship, train and plane ; they migrate ; and they settle in new locations and find new habitations. Some degenerate and get decimated or exterminated by other stronger languages ; some survive against the odds in tough environments ; some seem to fade out and then come back to life again ; and many in their turn

generate new languages. Like species, languages have ancestors and descendants. What's more, inter-relationships within the histories of language families, like those of species, tend to be conceptually modelled and visually mapped on *images of trees* (for example, Indo-European, Sino-Tibetan, Semitic, Austronesian, etc.), even though this model usually oversimplifies the shapes of mutually influencing languages from different groups.

5. Within any one language, poems, once expressed, are literally irrevocable but not necessarily recoverable. They can blow away on the wind and get lost. Poems belong ineluctably to the particular language in which they were first made. They grow in and from their speakers and writers to their listeners and readers through minds, voices, ears, eyes and hands. Languages in the minds, voices, ears, eyes and hands of their speakers, writers, listeners and readers are poems' necessary dwelling places. There ultimately exist no other *loci* for poems to live and flourish in – though in order to survive, they may need to pass (on, over) into a language other than the one they were made in.

6. Poems are not just decorative adornments for a language, prettifying but unnecessary adjuncts, patterns carved or engraved onto its surfaces. Proto-poems, with features such as reduplication, playful modulations of rhyme and assonance, and even simile, are made by small infants babbling in their cribs even as they approach and cross the borders into articulate speech. Ruth Weir notes : "[T]here are a great number of instances in the child's monologues where *play with the sounds of the language is basic in the hierarchy of language functions,* with other functions, be they referential or conative or metalingual, subordinated to it" (*emphasis added*).[10] The poetic function in language is not accidental, ornamental or artificial, but fundamental.

7. Whether in condensed or elaborated forms, mature poems express and encapsulate the power, delicacy and beauty of their language : they plummet its depths and scale its heights ; they test its limits, push its boundaries, and tap its possibly as-

yet-unrecognised and unregistered resources. Poems course through all the energetic pathways (meridians) of a language : through its taproot, tubers and rhizomes, along its trunk or main stem, into its boughs, branches, twigs, leaves, and meristematic tips. Poems transmit a language's spirit, soul, sap, vital energy : in Chinese, its *qi*.[11]

8.   Poems are the finest and purest forms of art that can be made in language. Whether composed and delivered orally or in writing, poems not only affirm and confirm the particular qualities – the unique genius – of the language they were made in, but they protect its life and guard its longevity. And once recorded, poems perpetuate their language. They defend it against its disintegration and death, against its passing into oblivion.

9.   In these ways, recorded poems offer a kind of *Sicherheit* to the language they're made in.[12] They ensure and insure it ; and for as long as that language lives, they endow its speakers with some measure of safety and security in inhabiting it, along with a sense of pride and confidence in it : that is, a sense of its stability, endurance, and durability. In all respects, then, poems are good for their language and for its speakers. Shelley said in *The Defence of Poetry* that poets are "the unacknowledged legislators of the world". Let it be added here that, rooted in language, poems are the unacknowledged protectors and guardians of humanity.

10.   Poems also enshrine dead languages, and bring something of them back to life again. Long after all its speakers have gone for good, recorded poems can guarantee our memory of a language and of those who once spoke it and lived in and through it. The discovery and decipherment of a poem recorded in a no-longer-spoken language will result in the resurrection of that language's spirit through the poem's textual translation into a currently living language. Consider, for example, the literatures of Sumerian, or Old Norse, and the insights we have today into those civilisations through translations of the Norse sagas and the Sumerian creation hymns. What's more, a poem recovered and resurrected from a

dead language may turn out to be a masterpiece, like the *Epic of Gilgamesh*, which lives on in a special kind of glory, despite the fact that nobody any longer speaks Sumerian or even knows for sure what it sounded like. Translated – transplanted – into many modern languages, a masterpiece like this, written over 4700 years ago, lives on, and in doing so, *challenges mortality.* Paradoxically, then, poems can survive their own languages. They also cross over many generations of human deaths. In this very real sense, then, poems defy and transgress death.

11. Both globally and in the particulate intimacy of *this* or *that*, poems continuously and energetically insist on thrusting life against death, creativity against destruction, and learning, memory and remembrance against ignorance, forgetting and oblivion. Whereas trees give us the oxygen that enables us to breathe, poems that grow from and through us, moving away from us on the wings of breath, also return inspiration to us by moving us. That is to say : in recycling inspiration to us, they re-inspire us. Poems recall us from exile into the radiant fulness of presence, isness, being, now-and-here.

12. A dendrology, a forest of tree-poems, is an emblem and manifestation of this spirit, these re-inspirations.

Riddling the Riddle

Twelve Propositions

1. A good riddle is *strange*. It's odd and curious and it's posed by a stranger, even one who may seem familiar. This stranger, familiar or not, is always *other*, *the* Other : curious, odd. And this stranger may be friendly or threatening, honest and sincere, or devious and beguiling : a potential friend or a dangerous enemy.

2. A riddle is part of a dialogue. Together with its answer, it can be a complete dialogue in itself.

3. A riddle is likely to occur in an encounter on a journey of discovery, in the context of a magical or mysterious narrative. A riddle is likely to be a question during a quest. It may be a test on a quest too. It often appears often out of nowhere. Or seems to. The riddler may be teacher, testing, teasing out response from a student..

4. A riddle is a mind-sharpener, a learning and liminal experience, a test before a door, gate, portal. The correct answer is the key or password to enable one to pass through, go further.

5. To pass the riddle's test means getting the key or pass to open the gate or door and pass through it and move on (up, down) to the next step or stage. To do this, the person who is asked the riddle (the traveller, *naif, ingénu*, beginner, novice, neophyte, wise child, etc.) *has* to answer it.

6. If the riddler seems threatening, the right answer can be a protection from further danger from that source, a more than effective weapon against that enemy : *Rumpelstiltskin*.[13]

7. A subtle and effective riddle challenges the mind to think in ways that surprise and delight. A riddle is ineluctably *heuristic*. Answering it opens up unforeseen, unimagined and even startling connections. A good riddle, if and when answered, reveals itself, its whole meaning and structure, in an "Aha !" Successfully an-

swering the riddle can give the traveller a start, a twinge, a shock : even a hint of heroism.

8. If a riddle's answer does arrive, it often does so with the suddenness of a lightning stroke. It presents (presences) both the present and the past – in the present. Like lightning, the sudden answer pierces through dark, mist, murk, haze – through apparent contradiction – through pretence and pretension – to open up (to) paradox, (to) the unexpected, even (to) a sparkling brightness, a numinous clarity.

9. Successfully answering a riddle cancels whatever seems to be *seemly* or *seeming, like* or *liked* or *likely*. It assembles the fragments of whatever was or might have been into what is and what is to follow : surprising. And to more questions, more puzzles, more riddles….

10. So : giving the right answer reveals, protects and projects. Perspectives widen, heighten, deepen.

11. Even so, a good riddle simultaneously requires and defies answering – like the famous Japanese *koan*, "What is the sound of one hand clapping ?" My probable-improbable answer to that one is : "Poetry."[14] Another perhaps even more possible-impossible reply might be "A riddle" or "Another riddle – *question mark ?*"

12. Sometimes a riddle has more than one right answer. Then, who knows, the riddled may even become the riddler.

Poetry and Midnight

Chiming the Hour

1. Beautiful midnight. At its chime, the soul's fingers play fugues on senses' organs in vaults of purest mind.

2. Things – remaining things – remain and fall away. They do so simultaneously. When they fall, what takes their place, inevitably, is music. The music of things as they are. When they stay, they tap their feet. They have no choice . And that's how it starts. They dance.

3. The music of things as they are recombines with the music of dream. In, through and out of dream. And with the underworld's music : sounds and depth-soundings. On instruments and through voices. Orchestrated and choired.

4. On a breath's oscillation, *I* disappears and returns. Faster, faster, on a pulse's. On a wave's white mane. No, quicker even than that – on the puff of a nano-second. On the breadth of a pico-tic.

5. Who would have thought it, thought *of* it ? That *I*, forgetting, *knows* this ? And has always known it ? *I*, in this constant ongoing dialogue with hordes of instant others ?

6. Hopkins knew this music in each thing's unique instress and inscape. He heard its pressures and strictures push through clouds and water whorls. Among minute particulars, Master Blake saw and heard it resonate (the) universal glory. These two I shall follow. These shall be my soul-guides.

7. All that's needed is breath. This heart is a transformer, pumping blood, breath, light. A time-breaker. A spacemaker.

8.   I could get drunk on this midnight. From this hearing that's a seeing, from this seeing that's a hearing. Oh you, most beautiful centre ! Oh you, most radiant core !

9.   And this *I* will *not* be obliterated. But deepened in this ground, be rooted all the more firmly. Like a springtime rowan tree in blossom, resting until dawn, and by July berrying in red clusters. And, no less, flying among stars. Brightly singing the dream.

10. After our ends, yours and mine, the singing and the dancing will go on, and on, without us. But in our time, this is no time for us to stop anything.

11. Even though any street at dawn – or field or forest or garden – will be hard to greet after this midnight, tender and terrible at once, steep generations of light will spread out from this blackness.

12. Rich-textured spangled quilt, blanketed now in cloudbank – matrix of all poems, yours is the blackest light, balancing the day's.[15]

Notes and References

EPIGRAPHS

1. William Blake. 'Jerusalem', 69, l. 42. In *Poetry and Prose of William Blake* (Geoffrey Keynes, ed.). London : The Nonesuch Library, 1956: p. 526.

2. Gerard Manley Hopkins, 'Parmenides'. In *Journals and Papers of Gerard Manley Hopkins* (Humphrey House, ed.). London, New York, Toronto : Oxford University Press, 1966 (1959), p. 127.

3. Gaston Bachelard, 'Poetic Instant and Metaphysical Instant'. In *Intuition of the Instant* (Rizo-Paton, Eileen, trans.). Evanston IL : Northwestern University Press, 2013 (1932), p. 60.

4. Dylan Thomas, 'In my Craft or Sullen Art'. In *Collected Poems 1934–1952*. London : J. M. Dent, 1957 (1952), p. 128.

5. Ted Hughes, 'The Thought Fox'. In *Selected Poems 1957–1967*. London : Faber and Faber, 1972, p. 9.

'POETRY AND MIDNIGHT : APPROACHING THE HOUR', pp. 7-9. Composed in 2020 and 2024.

'IMAGINATIONALISM', pp. 9-10. Composed 2016, 2024.

ON POETRY AND DREAM', pp. 11-13. Composed 2020, 2024.

'ON THE SPIRIT OF POETRY IN A TIME OF PLAGUE (THE FIRST IMAGINATIONALIST MANIFESTO)', pp. 14-16. Composed during the COVID pandemic, 2020.

'POETRY, TREES, AND HOPE', pp. 17-19, and 'A DENDROLOGY : ON LANGUAGE AND TREES', pp. 20-23. Composed, 2017–2018. These texts were written to accompany the performance of Silvia Pio's Italian translation of the 365-line chant poem TREE (ALBERO) at the *Festa degli Alberi* (*Festival of Trees*) in Mondovì, Piedmont, Italy (1 October 2017). Accompanying the publication of TREE in several languages in *Margutte*, they inaugurate the *Albero Project*, an ongoing multilingual collection of ecopoetic texts. See 'The Albero Project : Index', online.

'RIDDLING THE RIDDLE', pp. 24-25. Composed 2024.

'POETRY AND MIDNIGHT : CHIMING THE HOUR'. pp. 26-27. Composed in 2020 and 2024. Dedicated to Paul Scott Derrick.

1. This echoes : "Poetry is a challenge to mortality and a criticism of Death" (*Imagems* 1, Shearsman, Bristol, 2013 : p. 8) – a previous response to Matthew Arnold's dictum : "Poetry is a criticism of life."

2. See the anonymous English medieval poem *Perle*. Like so many other poems, its oyster is a dream. See *Pearl*, ed. E. V. Gordon, The Clarendon Press, Oxford, 1953.

3. Latin *anima* 'soul' is only half the story. In some Indo-European languages, vowels such as [*a*], [*a*] and [*æ*]and syllables such as [*an*] and [*am*] enact and epitomise not only 'breath' but also 'call' ('speech'). This suggests that the condition of 'ensoulment' means whatever or whoever *breathes* and has *voice*. Consider also : Sanskrit *ātmán* 'soul, spirit, self, essence, being' ; Greek ἀτμός (*atmós*) 'vapour, steam, smoke' ; ἄνεμος (*ánemos*) 'wind' ; Old English *æpm* 'breath' ; German *Atem* 'breath', *atmen* 'breathe' ; Dutch *adem* 'breath'.

4. Osip Mandelstam, 'About an Interlocutor'. In *Selected Essays*, trans. Sidney Monas, University of Texas Press, Austin, TX, 1977, pp. 63 and 64.

5. Anthony Rudolf, *Wine from Two Glasses (Poetry and Politics : Trust and Mistrust in Language)*. Adam Archive Publications, Kings College, London, 1991, pp. 45 and 48.

6. The word *anthology* combines Greek ἄνθος 'flower' and λόγος 'principle of coherence or order'. The word is "…of multiple origins. Partly a borrowing from Greek. Partly a borrowing from French. Partly a borrowing from Latin. Partly formed within English, by compounding." *OED* online.

7. From Greek δέντρο (*déntro*) 'tree'.

8. *OED* online.

9. The 'dendrology' mentioned here is the ongoing *Albero Project*, which Silvia Pio and I founded in 2017. See the note on 'POETRY, TREES, AND HOPE', p. 28 above.

10. See Ruth Hirsch Weir, *Language in the Crib*, Mouton and Co., The Hague, 1962, p. 103. On language play, see *ibid.* pp. 102-106, 108-109 and 146.

11. *Qi* 'energy, life-energy' (traditional Chinese 氣, simplified Chinese 气). See Zhang Yu Huan and Ken Rose, *A Brief History of Qi*, Paradigm Publications, Brookline, MA, 2001. The meridians are the pathways or

channels that conduct the flow of *qi* in the human body, as influenced in acupuncture.

12. *Sicherheit* : a German noun that includes most of the ideas expressed in English words such as *surety, assurance, safety, security,* etc., as well as, by association, *comfort, stability, dependability,* etc.

13. See also 'Riddles Wisely Expounded', the first section in Volume 1 of *The English and Scottish Popular Ballads,* collected and edited by Francis James Child, Dover Publications, New York, 1965 (1882), pp. 1-5.

14. See RB, *Imagems 1,* Shearsman Books, Bristol, 2013, p. 10.

15. See the sequence 'Black Light : poems in memory of George Seferis'. In RB, *For the Living : Selected Longer Poems 1965–2000,* Shearsman Books, Exeter, 2011.